ETHNOGRAPHIC POETIC TRANSCRIPTIONS ON THE LIFE-WORLD

OF FOUR AFRICAN AMERICAN MEN

by

Dr. James O. Richardson

University of West Florida

Submitted for possible presentation at the 2007 annual meeting of

The Mid-South Sociological Association

Order this book online at www.trafford.com
or email orders@trafford.com

Most Trafford titles are also available at major online book retailers.

Printed in the United States of America.

ISBN: 978-1-4669-9560-4 (sc)
ISBN: 978-1-4669-9559-8 (e)

Library of Congress Control Number: 2013909276

Trafford rev. 05/17/2013

 www.trafford.com

North America & international
toll-free: 1 888 232 4444 (USA & Canada)
phone: 250 383 6864 ♦ fax: 812 355 4082

ABSTRACT

POETIC TRANSCRIPTIONS ON THE LIFE-WORLD
OF FOUR AFRICAN AMERICAN MEN:
VOICE, GENRE, AND CARE

My purpose is to unveil the relation between poetic transcriptions and qualitative research. This process is how we make sense of ourselves, and perhaps, a doorway towards understanding the *other*. Poetic transcriptions requires being prepared for the *other* to speak to us, thus treating the *other* as equals to be met, not objects to be inspected, tolerated, or unseen. As I endeavored to examine their meanings and truths, my poetic transcriptions are about the dreams deferred, silenced voices and hidden faces of four African American men. My poetic transcriptions are dialogues about authentic Blackness and about what is, or ought to be.

Introduction

Blacks continue to be disproportionate underrepresented within academic landscape. Despite being marginalized and oppressed Black people have contributed to poetic discourses and yet are not fully recognized among social researchers. My poetic transcriptions though focus on Black perspectives that frequently have been overlooked and silenced. Blacks' poetic transcriptions are usually grounded in a life-world of Blackness, often challenge Whites' assumptions about Black identity and counter the dominant views of Whites privilege. Blacks' poetic transcriptions are expressions of contradictions in the lives of Blacks and portrayals of their reality between two worlds as exploited but somehow delivered and as undesirables but somehow free.

Paradoxically though, African Americans poetic transcriptions reflect a life-world of in-between-ness, a world between hopes and dreads and a world between lost prayers and doubts. Repeatedly, African Americans' poetic transcriptions contradict Whites' ideas of equality, and justice. Blacks distressing but authentic poetic transcriptions are quest journeys through occupied territory of White privilege and troubled seas of racism, and at times, fixated on otherworldliness. Thus, poetic transcriptions are a progression toward becoming a complete and whole person by focusing on moral or ethical dilemmas of race.

Although poetic transcriptions are day-to-day lived experiences of Black people, they are useful and artful inquiries of self-inquiry, storytelling and semi-structured interviews. At some level though, poetic transcriptions involve challenging the oppressive social structure and the rejection of previously held notions of Blackness. Black poetic transcriptions invite African Americans to explore their transformative Black moments or meaningful turning points of a Black consciousness, while effectively seeking to change Whites' bigotry and indifference.

In addition, poetic transcriptions are a pedagogy that connect personal agency to critical thinking, and thus are a process of learning and constructing knowledge that permit the oppressed to examine the contextually of their positionality. Finally, poetic transcriptions are representations of reality about the marginalized *other*, and outsiders in the form of poetry and narratives.

What is Poetic Transcription?

Poetic transcription is an imaginative style of writing used by researchers to illustrate lived experiences or a life-world of the participants. This is a fresh postmodernist type of writing that fully materialized in the 1980's and allows African American researchers to exemplify and to tell about their perplexities in new ways. Poetic transcription also involves a willingness to give birth to a new sort of narrative meaningfulness, but despite its newness, it has sometimes been seen as absurdity.

Poetic transcription manages to give voice to individuals in additional to power by transforming them into rhythmic agents of narration (Carr, 2003). Thus these narratives are inspired message that is poetically structured and are usually reflective, sensitive, and nostalgic in nature.

Poetic transcriptions articulate the inexpressible and are intended to stimulate readers' reactions and constructive representations. Its significance is often cloaked in colloquialisms and everyday language that illuminate lived experiences, including contradictions.

Poetic transcription is recognized as investigative writing that presents qualitative data in poetic forms. It is the usage of interview data transcribed into poetic expressions, virtually in the form of free verse (Carr, 2003). Poetic transcription is particularly appealing and useful when one is looking for imagery, metaphors or symbols. For example, a poetic transcription may dramatically and poignantly represent such phenomena as power, loneness, oppression, poverty and gender inequality (Larkin, 2007). Sometimes poetic transcription can be an undertaking about understanding injustice, the impact of racism and standing with the powerless in the world as eyewitnesses. Furthermore it can express our dilemmas (Willits, 2007). Finally, because students come from many different cultures, postmodernists' teachers can even use poetic transcriptions to allow their students to construct assignments that convey their feelings about their life-world and lived experiences (Sweeney, 2007).

Purpose of Poetic Transcription

From a postmodernism perspective, the very nature of poetic transcription is its authenticity and individual style of expression makes it nearly impossible to classify. According to Berger and Luckman (1966) The Social Construction of Reality, the sociology of knowledge (coined by Max Scheler during the 1920's) must concern itself with what ever passes for knowledge in a society, regardless of the ultimate validity or invalidity of such knowledge. "Sociology of knowledge" must seek to understand the processed by which knowledge is transmitted and maintained; it is also concerned with the analysis of the social construction of reality.

Poetic transcription is one of many ways "Sociology of knowledge" is transmitted, but has been generally disregarded by social scientists until lately because of their partiality for objective data rather than for feelings, personal experiences and narratives. It has also been unnoticed because of the prevailing belief that the subjective approach cannot be authenticated, corroborated or validated. While poetic transcription is a creative perception of a phenomenon articulated through meaning, it is a constructed reality of everyday life that is shared with others. It is also a reflection of an individual's social constructed reality, his role in his surroundings and himself as he experienced it. Although poetic transcription is a form of action research characterize by the use of poetic imagery, it is but commonsense knowledge we share with others in the normal, self-evident routines of everyday life.

Commonsense knowledge rather than ideas must be the central focus for the "Sociology of knowledge". It is precisely this knowledge that constitutes the fabric of meanings without which no society could exist. Therefore "Sociology of knowledge" must concern itself with the social construction of reality. If the reality of everyday life is to be understood, account must be taken of its local character. The reality of everyday life is taken for granted as reality, and does not require additional verification over and beyond its simple presence. It is simple there, as self-evident and compelling facts of authenticity about the restrictive conditions of an individual human life.

Poetic transcription is a qualitative and fictive approach that symbolizes or refers to one's everyday life-world. It evaluates and endeavors to understand uncertainties and changes from one's standpoint. The literal meaning of an expression is cloaked with embellishment, in one's imagination, personal knowledge and particularly in cases where there is no knowledgeable and factual interpretation of one's lived experience. Poetic transcription is an imaginative awareness of an experience expressed through meaning and rhythmic language choices so as to stir up an emotional reaction. Perhaps poetic transcription is a way of keeping outsiders out and sometimes even keeping this radical phenomenology hidden. There is a problem however of keeping out the outsiders from the true meaningfulness and at the same time having them acknowledge the legitimacy of this practice; the insiders, on the other hand, have to be kept in by the use of implied words.

Poetic transcription is an early form of writing that has gone through many and radical reinvention over time and can bestow new meaning to language so that historical events can be reinterpreted without necessarily upsetting the institutional order. The communication of meanings is based on one's social location and constructed reality. These meanings may, to outsiders, appear to have dubious functionality and serve no useful purpose at all during other times. Because individuals and their personalities cannot be effectively understood apart from their particular social framework in which they were shaped, poetic transcription has been known to employ rhymes and stanzas, but this is by no means essential.

A Black writer's poetic transcription is reflective of his everyday life-world and presents itself as a reality interpreted and subjectively meaningful to him as a logical world of reality. Among the multiple realities

there is a dominant one that presents itself as the reality pre-eminent.
For example, every individual is born into an objective social structure
within which he encounters the significant others who are in charge of
his socialization. These significant others and their definition of him are
imposed on him as objective reality. Thus a Black lower-class individual not
only absorbs a Black lower-class perspective of the social world, he absorbs
it in the discoloration given him by his parents. This perspective may induce
a disposition of satisfaction, acceptance, antagonism, or nonconformity.

Poetic transcription may enlighten outsiders about how the Black
child perceives himself, others and his environment, and may produce a
ground theory. The Black lower-class child will not only come to inhabit
a world greatly different from that of a White upper-class child, but may
do so in a manner quite different from the Black lower-class child next
door. Socialization takes place under circumstances that are highly charged
emotionally. There is a good reason to believe that without such emotional
attachment to the significant others the learning process would be complex
if not impossible. Internalization occurs only as identification occurs and
the Black child takes on the role and attitudes, that is, internalizes them and
makes them his own.

The oppressed individual becomes what he is addressed as by his
significant others and he learns who he is by what he is called. Every name
implies a nomenclature, which in turn implies a designated social location.
To be given an identity involves being assigned a specific place in the world
where one belongs or ought to belong. The individual apprehends himself
as being both inside and outside of his society. As Patricia Hills Collins
indicates, he is seen and at the same time, he is not seen. This implies that
the individual must always create and mimic what is expected of him as an

outsider in order to be accepted. The relationship between the individual and the objective social world is like a constant balance act of fervently yearning to be an accepted of society and the same time maintain his human dignity. This unfair disadvantage inherent in the circumstances of being a Black child has noticeable effect because it is the African-American adult who set the rules of the game in order to succeed and survive. The child can play the game with eagerness or with angry opposition but unfortunately, there is no other game in around.

Since the child has no choice in the selection of his significant others, his identification with adults is quasi-automatic. For the same reason, his internalization of his particular reality is quasi-inevitable. The Black child does not necessarily internalize the world of his significant others as one of many possible worlds as a White child does. The Black child internalizes his world as the only possible world. Poetic transcription thus enhances our understanding of the Black child's primary socialization process, in that it achieves what may be seen as the most significant confidence scam that society plays on the Black child. Consequently, this socialization practice makes it appear that a life-world of poverty and inferiority is a certainty, but this process is only a fact of circumstances and a collection of unpleasant incidents, and thus to make consequential the horrible accident of his birth.

It is the kind of language and narratives that must be internalized above all and by means of them, various motivational and interpretative schemes are internalized as institutionally defined. These schemes provide the Black child with institutional programs for everyday life, some immediately applicable to him, others anticipating conduct socially defined for later in life. These programs are immediately appropriate and anticipatory that distinguishes his identity of Blackness. This is why the language of poetic transcription is critical for deconstruction; it disrupts or unsettle taken for granted concepts, and seeks to reveal invalid assumptions.

Consequently, poetic transcription is a type of narrative ethics, which highlights the meaning of individuality, the virtues of character, and the individual and shared narratives. Poetic transcription is also contextual in that the meaning of a particular language can only be appreciated in the specific perspective in which it unfolds. Understanding poetic transcription requires being prepared for the *Other* to speak to us (thus treating the *Other* as a human being to be met and not an object to be viewed, tolerated, oppressed or ignored) and recognizing that dialogue and conversation are the conditions in which understanding emerge (Schwandt, 2001).

From a postmodernism perspective, poetic transcription may articulate social problems such as the reification of social reality and its anxiety of human phenomena as if they were things, that is, in non-human. It implies that man is capable of forgetting his own soul and the souls of others. In Berger's construction, reification is interpreted as a state of amnesia in which the individual "forgets" the human origins of the social world. This "forgetfulness" is explained, in turn, as a defensive reaction by which the individual seeks to establish psychic stability in the face of "some fundamental terrors of human existence, notably the terror of chaos" (Berger and Pullberg, 1966).

The reified world is, by description, a dehumanized and oppressive life world and accordingly, poetic transcription may also describe African-Americans' lived experiences as a strange reality over which he has no power. Even while understanding the world in reified terms, some of them continue to recreate it for themselves. Paradoxically, others are able of producing a reality that "Reification" in this context becomes a derogatory label and uncritically take the existing social order and institutions as incentives for self-actualization. However, many African-Americans are yet reduced to functioning as representatives or "personifications" of the things in their possession (Scheler, 1967).

The process of Writing Poetic Transcriptions

My poetic transcriptions are based upon conversations, interviews, and dialogue with the participants; they are sophisticated, flowing, yet simple, rich with symbols and hidden truths about the life-world of the four men. In writing these poetic transcriptions, I looked back on a forgotten, self-contained Black community and life-world of warmth, safety and closeness. My endeavor was a holistic journey of self-discovery between the past and the present, between modernism and postmodernism, between Paul Lawrence Dunbar and Langston Hughes, and between Black pride and humility. I looked back, as well as forward; I yearn for the Black community as it was back then and so long ago. As I reflected on my lived experience black then, I equivocated between nostalgia of family intimacy and Jim Crow, between outdated text books and integration, between closeness of neighbors, but now strangers and in many ways adversaries.

My Poetic transcriptions sought to capture subjective experiences and feelings of the participants rather than objective data that produce a central function in unfolding individuals' feelings and particularly with regard to pathological expressions. My Poetic transcriptions portrayed meaningfulness in subtle and elusive ways and or made the unknown

15

visible; they became bridges between the authentic and the imaginary and a journey into the human soul; their narratives were a way to perceive the personal and subjective world of the participants. Even unconscious elements of individuals' experiences require insight, sensitivity and self-reflection. Poetic transcriptions ought to compel one to surrender preconceptions and egocentric attitudes.

As a researcher, I assumed that the participants believed what they articulated and that there was a measure of reasonable reliability in their thinking. I also assumed and had to assume, that the participants' responses to questions that they would not normally answer. Over the years, they too, faced dilemmas that are unknown to outsiders and yet they prospered during of Jim Crow. The life-world of these men cannot be appreciated without taking into account the complexity between their lived experiences of survival and shared hope.

There is a strange relationship between poetic transcriptions and qualitative research. Poetic transcription is a process of how we see the world and make sense of ourselves. This paper affords the unique opportunity of contributing in a real way an increased understanding of human experiences from a Black perspective and frequently poetic writers' perspectives are reflective of their circumstances, nurturing and real-life experience. Simple words, natural style, and sense making of absurdities are examples of the essence of poetic transcription (Foley, 2005).

Therefore, the words of poetic transcriptions are not mine alone. The participants' eyes speak with plurality of meaning about an authentic life-world and the type of persons they are to be taken to be, or the nature of the group in which they claim membership. They alone are the interpreters and consequently there are no systematically set of codes of interpretations. Poetic transcriptions are there merely to be understood, thus the interpretations of poetic transcriptions should not be subjected to the criteria of scientific examination.

Poetic transcriptions are riddles and scientific inquiry cannot solve riddles. They are riddles, precisely, because, to understand, the understander must be familiar with the metaphorical and figurative language. Outsiders usually look for responses in the world of referents. But when they can't find the answer there, they become increasingly aware that poetic transcriptions are a riddle. Thus, they look for other possibilities even if the riddle is presented out loud. Insiders should discern this. They should know about riddles, the expressions, the sound structure, the grammatical form and the meanings in a multiplicity of additional linguistic perspective (Tsur, 2000). For the understander, solving the riddle is the only way out, but sometimes the understander must stay behind.

In essence, poetic narratives/ transcriptions are intellectual spaces and serve social functions of empowerment. They encourage agency, praxis and ethics and provide underlying theoretical models of race and class; they also have particular meaning about language that can only be understood from the specific perspectives whereby they explain phenomena. For instance, though Black folktales were the primary means African Americans communicated to one another back then, poetic transcriptions/narratives have altered the ways in which Black scholars articulate their dilemmas.

Regularly, African Americans are portrayed as part of a collectivity whole and yet live a dual existence of collective and personal experiences; therefore are irreducible to each other so that an unresolved tension exists and at the same time there is shared life-world. Because poetic transcriptions capture dilemmas, they are outside of everyday language; actually though, they are visual images of ideas where words are series of signs signifying meaning of conflicting values. Poetic transcriptions are not only journeys of discovering and knowing, but a different kind of knowing. This approach attempts to deconstruct reality, address grand narratives, social injustice and ethical responsibility.

Poetic transcription is a form of writing that allows the *voices* of those researched to express both individual and collective experience in succinct and distinctive ways by cutting across arbitrary divisions between public and private, objective and subjective experiences. This form of writing not only offers wider audiences for academic writing about the life-world of others but is also potentially liberating for those within the academic context who wish to read and construct qualitative research in different format. Poetic transcription is a progression of transformation and human inquiry where understanding the *other* becomes far-reaching (Debra, 2004).

Despite the fact that poetic transcription has a wider meaning for both academic and public discourse and offers a holistic framework which can be utilized in diverse ways by researchers, it also provides first-hand knowledge of how people define themselves and construct their life-world. Poetic transcription is an academic storytelling and learning these stories is often produced through in-depth interviews with participants. These stories often inform readers about an unknown or a hidden life-world; some times, they are imaginary tales portraying the world as an orderly but chaotic place of *"ought's"* and *"should's."* This form of research writing that can offer empowering representations for feminist researchers as well (Debra, 2004).

Poetic transcriptions can embrace shared experiences of *otherness*, and sense making, which is a growing awareness of the *other* lived experiences and life-world. The *other* is the lone interpreter of his/her lived experience and therefore there are no systematically set of codes of interpretations for researchers. For the *other*, poetic transcriptions are there merely to be understood and should not be subjected to the criteria of scientific examination. The *other* can articulate the kind of person he/she is to be taken to be, or the character of the group in which she/he claims membership. Often, and unconsciously, the *other*'s eyes subtly verbalize voices of *otherness*.

Pedagogy of Resistance

While it is beyond the scope of poetic transcriptions, I did not undertake to offer a comprehensive dialogue of resistance theory; however, I discovered a relationship between poetic transcriptions and resistance. Poetic transcription can and do embrace resistance theory which is grounded in the notion that the oppressed have a degree of agency that allows them to activity oppose the structures of domination in various ways. Like other similar inspired writings poetic transcriptions may well provide insight against forms of dehumanization and expose ways in which inequalities are duplicated over and over again. What many have downplayed or disregarded is the reality that oppressed groups have produced critical ways of learning that have been transformed and lived out (Denzin and Lincoln, 2003).

Historically, the African American community served as a significant example of this by establishing a strong critical tradition of both theory and practice in educational institutions which they innocently advanced long before the advance of critical theory by the Frankfurt School or the rise of critical pedagogy as practiced by Freire. For instance, Black folk tales and African folk lore used narratives of animals, metaphors and symbols to obscure the real meaning of their reality. In doing so, they theorized about their conditions as a people who were racially and culturally dominated. Consequently, the African American intellectuals of the early twentieth century developed a scholarly and intellectual poetic transcription tradition that was different from their ancestors (Jennings and Lynn, 2005).

Education and Poetic Transcriptions

Today, education prompts us to accept established knowledge, and it is not clear how traditional education should be understood from the standpoint of the oppressed, (Roth, 2006). Poetic transcriptions may provide new ways of perceiving that knowledge from a different standpoint, but this method maybe problematic and may not be intellectually recognized as a qualitative framework. In the past however, this diversity was ignored or stifled by modernity. Anyone who deviated from this framework of normalcy was subject to exclusion, marginalization, silencing, or assimilation. Currently, many Black writers are not willing to be silenced, excluded, or even assimilated and yet, they are asserting a politics of recognition and more inclusiveness (Roth, 2006).

The awareness of Blackness is unconditional. Black children are forced to use mainstream languages in education settings, but they tend to retain and use language they have internalized, identified with, and acquired whatever language spoken around them. It is an interesting phenomenon in early language attainment that Black children seem to depend more on what is said rather than on how it is said. Modern textbooks revealed this duality but then dismissed it. One's identity and understanding are influenced by linguistic practices outside and within cultures. Consequently, educational institutions can no longer embrace the thought that learning particular principles can be legitimized only by linguistic practices.

Poetic Transcription and Agency

Poetic transcription provides insightful animation about the life-world and lived experiences of the four participants. Like hermeneutic of suspicious, my poetic transcriptions seek to unmask false consciousness by disclosing hidden feelings through illustrations and caricatures. Although my poetic transcriptions may produce a sense of agency for some who feel a sense powerless, it is nevertheless a collaborative understanding of the lived experiences of the four men. Occasionally, poetic transcriptions twist and alter cultural reproduction like a distorted mirror; they change reality but paradoxically and eventually producing a cultural pedagogy. My poetic transcriptions made use of the men's voices with the expectation that they would stimulate self-awareness. Poetic transcriptions often require an interpretation of data in a particular way; it also sequesters hermeneutics and dispute modernist's interpretation and meaning (Denzin and Lincoln, 2003).

In addition, my poetic transcriptions maybe a postmodernist's window into the souls and personal lives of many individuals. Although poetic transcription can be a reflection of multiple and contradictory realities, it expressed a particular class, gender, racial and cultural perspective. Poetic transcription is also many things to many people and often cloaks and frames hidden saying. Persistently, my transcriptions is a reexamination and questioning of power and privilege; like a prism, it discloses and simplifies modernist notions, and alters the appearance of equality by showing a dissimilar worldview through the eyes of the oppressed. My poetic transcription normalizes, corrects, and put slices of truth together, as well as brings psychological and emotional unity to an interpretative understanding (Jennings and Lynn, 2005).

Conclusion

Before I begin to illustrate my poetic transcriptions, I must make one more observation. Poetic transcription involves the use of comparative cases analysis, personal experience, interview data, and self-reflection with the anticipation of making the life-world of the four men visible. I expected to obtain a better understanding of the most common themes and to transmit the hopes, fears, needs and goals of the four participants. Finally, I cannot explain the meaningfulness of my poetic transcriptions and claim that my premise is correct if they agree with the practice of those in power. Poetic transcriptions must in some way be qualitatively internalized and become a habit of the heart.

Poetic transcriptions:

#1

At one time,

We were just plain _____ Old colored folks

To just plain colored

We went from Black to Blue

To all shades of colors _____ and all shades of hue

We went from Negro to Black _____ To just plain Black

To Black is beautiful

With our Afros _____

We went from Sambo or Mammy _____ Without a name

To selling our souls _____ to playing the game

We went from slavery to uncle Toms

From blackface _____ to pretend

Preferring to be white _____ while we grin

We went from African to Maroon

To Quadroon to Creole _____ and couldn't fit in

Yet,

We placed our hopes _____ Therein.

We went from passing for White _____ Dreaming to be free

While brothers were Dying _____

From that same oak tree!

2

<u>We were one back then</u>

Fictive family members

Borrowing sugar

Rice and flour,

And

Even clothes _____ On special occasions

Appreciation _____

Gently and clearly

Was always unspoken,

Back Then!

Generosity and caring

Was our life-world _____ Back then.

While

Survivorship, deepen.

And

Nurtured Relationships

Shaped our identity

And

Our humanity.

Back then,

But nowadays,

Longed ____ and ____ Buried!

Dismissed, ____ and _____ Dismantled.

We are . . . . Simply,

Alienated . . . . Beings

Hiding authenticity

In private enclaves

But dare not lose

Our artificial face!

#3

Black Jesus,

White Jesus

Brown or blue

You have to love me!

Before he loves you.

Maybe,

He left before slavery,

Or

Long _____ before Katherine

Maybe,

He left before the riots

Or

Even Jim Crow

Maybe,

He took the interstate

Escaping the ghettoes

And fled! _____

High rent and rats, and Toxic waste

And maybe

Police brutality

Come by here lord!

Come by here.

He ain't here just now,

He left long ago ____

He ain't picking cotton,

Not now,

Not any more.

Disappeared,

Vanished!

Gone!

to the Suburbs.

#4

They articulate,

We are all brothers below the skin

But you can see them

Authenticating themselves

By pulling on their skin

While looking suspiciously,

At yours.

They may, embrace you _____

in their prayers,

and say, _____

The power of God

Is near!

While pointing in one direction

And making sure _____

You scurry for another.

5

I think _____ it is

Remarkable,

In this belatedly postmodern world

The invention of Blackness

Marginalized.

Our lives and lived experiences

of God.

Our striving,

Our longing _____ for the Spirit,

Our cries and moans

Stigmatized

Hiding God's greatness and image

From of us!

6

Some have discerned our absence

From their life-world,

and this

Has trouble them _____

For not utilizing the master's tools.

With appalling accuracy

They have eradicated!

7

For many Black Americans

The American dream

Is customarily found

In declining pay checks,

Welfare lines, lottery games,

Or the Fantasy five

But only for whose

Who survive!

#8

It's just a game.

Selling our souls

For riches and fame.

Denying the truth, we play the game

and go right on with tears and sighs

Seeking a dream filled with lies

Acting all White!

to please the man

It where our dreams

Falls or stands!

#9

African Americans

have Ignored

or disregarded

A Fundamental reality

That, _____ We!

Black people,

Learned, _____ Back then!

in school,

or Perhaps,

At home _____ Sharing!

      # 10

Who am I?

Am I the infant

You conceived

When you raped my mama

Or,

the infant You snatched!

From her breast _____

and sold me

Down

The

Mississippi . . . .

Am I the boy?

Advertised

From your auction blocks

Who ran away?

Caught!

Beaten.

And

Stripped

Am I the young man,

Who built your mansions?

And

Ploughed your fields?

Am I the old man

who

Erected your libraries,

Raised your children

And

fought your wars?

Am I,

Now ___

Your tormentor

A beast to be to be feared,

Between your

Nightmares

And

Haunting fears?

11

Our disquieting propensity

To treat God as "White"

And

Thus,

have yielded to idolatry

That

Suggest _____

Merely

That we have

Disenchantly

Lost our way

12

<u>A White man's nostalgic</u>

My mama

Never fixed me a biscuit

Old colored woman

Always did

My mama

Never seemed to care

Old colored woman,

Always did

Didn't know where

The old colored woman lived

Or ever went _____

I've missed those biscuits

Ever since!

I loved that colored woman

She never complained

Didn't know her family nor her name

That Old colored woman

Used to make me smile

But _____

She was a Nigger, All awhile.

My mama

Never fixed me a biscuit

Old colored woman

Always did

I was a somebody!

Even though, a kid.

13

Our mother

had us two children

Because of her wits end

Our grandmother took us in.

Fed, clothed and almost died,

While praying to God with tears and sighs.

She didn't give birth, _____ but gave us life

We'll never forgot her sacrifice!

My daddy, I suppose, ____

Left longed before

Leaving us two children . . . . with nowhere to go

My mother, at her wits ends

Could not find a neighbor

or perceive a friend.

It was our grandmother

Who gave us all!

Who nurtured and loved us

So we wouldn't fall

Our mother had us two children

I never thought it so . . . .

To have a daddy

You never loved . . . .

And . . . . never got . . . . to know!

14

You call me Brother?

You call me brother?

Amidst hate and lies

Unappreciated and marginalized

And

You call me brother?

You sponge and scrounge

and forget all kindness

And

You call me brother?

You snoop and gossip

and know not what

and you call me brother?

My name and character

You quickly scandalize

Whatever is told is no surprise

And

You call me brother?

You wreck and destroy whatever is mine

proposed not a cent,

not even a dime

And

You call me brother?

Mouth and hands are visible woes

Ignoring your brother, they are always closed

Rumors and hearsay and disregarded reality

It's your brother, you cannot see

You forget you owe,

While your balance _____

is Overdue

It means little, concerning you.

Instead of trusting and treating me kind

You prefer scheming, decadence and lying

And

You call me Brother?

#15

We used to be

We used to be Black! _____ Real Black!

Black as the darkest nights . . . .

and Black as the Mississippi blues

We suffered and died, _____ and paid our dues.

We used to be Black, _____ real Black!

We used to be proud with friends abound,

Now, _____ we are nothing more

than the White man's clown.

We used to be Black.

Real _____ Black!

16

How does one survive under oppression,

or 39 slashes to the back?

How does one survive hatred

without truly fighting back?

How does one survive subjugation

and denied at every turn?

How does one survive prejudices

without any chance to learn?

How does one survive White privilege?

Yet, it has no name,

How do Blacks become free

Without in fact, going insane!

17

I must give back, to help and improve

To Show my affection and gratitude.

My Pain and suffering may never be told

But My feeble gift . . . may save a soul!

I must give back, as I perceive,

Much was given, and much received.

Family, mentors and also friends

That was my gift . . . . Back then!

To pay my dues not by words or smiles

It's my goal to work and strive

It's a duty and honorable task

To assist the needed and all who ask

Deeply thankful! _____,

Some went lack that is why . . . .

I must give back!

To my community, neighbor and town

To those who are weak,

And to those who are down.

     # 18

How does it feel to be an insider within?

Though they accepted our behavior,

They judged our skin!

How does it feel?

To wear our stigmatized face

Knowing in fact

We have no place.

How does it feel?

To often dream

We'll be heard and

hopefully seen.

How does it feel?

To be a marginalized _____ Self!

Dehumanized _____ until nothing is left.

How does it feel?

When we are all alone,

Dreaming of a world where we belong.

How does it feel?

To longed for a place

And to ultimately put off

Our Jim Crow face!

Perhaps,

It's to our shame,

If we fail our task!

Discovered!

Caught!

Without our masks!

We must bear in mind,

Cinderella went home

Late into the night,

However, deprived,

She was beautiful . . . .

and Black!

#19

Whites

Nurtured on milk

of White supremacy

Rocked to sleep

By the hands of hatred

And tightly Held

in the arms of malice

Taught!

"Lay me down to sleep"

A Black mammy

Arranged your bed

While you rested

Your racist's head

But now _____

She's gone

And now _____

She's dead!

20

We wear the masks!

We wear our masks

To cover our faults

And to hide our **fears**

We wear our smiles without frets or **tears**

We wear our masks!

We wear our masks . . . . To cover our weakness

And to hide our **pain**

So . . . .

We keep . . . . on . . . . smiling

And playing the **game**

We wear our masks!

We wear our masks . . . . So we can **be**

Something we are not

But afraid . . . . to **see!**

We wear our masks!

We wear our masks . . . . Even though

They are not **real**

Hiding us from love . . . .

So we can't **feel!**

    # 21

Will your dream lingers **on**

And slowly . . . . fades away and **die**

To make you sad and **mourn**

And **cry!**

And yet . . . . filled with love

Your heart, mind and **soul**

Have kindness to give

And a love . . . . **untold!**

Will your dreams . . . . slowly disappear

And increasingly . . . . fall **away**

Like a vivid and lively flower

That dries up . . . .

And **decay!**

Will your dreams . . . . cause you

To once again

Live!

To bring you joy

With all the love you have

And with all

Your love

To give!

22

We failed to understand

We are a people in a blessed land

Fearful of outsiders and those within

Suspicious of our neighbors and closest friends

Acknowledged experience and unseen events

We have constructed and if not invented

While mysterious persons are commonly taken away

We worship regularly and piously pray

Caricatures are created for those we distrust

They are not Christians and unlike us

Our mechanical mind made security our goal

But hatred and fright have taken its toil

Our doors are locked and so are our minds

Have welcome cruelty of every kind

Our number one enemy . . . . is no less than us

On our coin . . . . "In god we trust"

We are not the citizens we used to be

Who loved freedom and liberty . . . .

A fearless people filled with self esteem

For many nations . . . . that was their dream

But now we . . . . are and it is sad . . . . to say

We have had our greatest day

Too many of us failed to discerned

That humility is a gift . . . . we refuse to learn

23

<u>What breaks my heart</u>?

Mothers . . . . whose child

Unable to read, cannot write

Never known a kiss or a sweet good night

Deserted and neglected, they only discern

Love and joy, they failed to learn

Forsaken souls, abandoned and left alone

Jails and prisons their only homes

They are dumped onto school playgrounds

Like . . . . sad little creatures!

Or miserable . . . . looking clowns

Like fiends or beasts . . . . They go untamed

To hate or kill, it's all a game

       Thus,

To live and die . . . . They only feed

On the weak, the poor and those in need

What's break my heart?

Is a child untrained!

To live in ignorance all his days

He exploits others

Without something in return

Always a victim

He never learns!

24

Wake me . . . . When it's over

When my dreams . . . . indeed comes true

Wake me when it's over

When . . . . I am silently in your arms

Holding you

Wake me . . . . when it's over

Then . . . . I'll truly learn to feel

To discern . . . . your love is right

And to know . . . . your love is real!

Wake me . . . . when it's over

So my tears may no longer flow

When you bestow your love

Forever more!

Wake me . . . .

When it's over

When my darkness . . . . turns to day

When you are here . . . . To cherish

And to hold . . . . and

To always stay!

Wake me!

When

It's over . . . .

#25

Some Things

Some things . . . . Are a gift

But some things . . . . One must **strive**

But it is your love . . . . I highly **prize!**

Some things . . . . Are sometimes

       Not for sale

While other things . . . . are **free**

But I'll endeavor . . . . For your love

Throughout . . . . **eternity**

       Some things

Come . . . . At a great **cost!**

For . . . . it is your love . . . . And my dreams

I dreadfully . . . . **lost!**

Some things

I'll attempt . . . . until the **end**

To revive your love and to bring you back

       again!

Some things . . . . Were never meant to **be**

But . . . . it's my love . . . . I want to **see**

Sometimes . . . . Though

There are many disappointments

Even . . . . discarded **tears**

Yet . . . . My heart

And my love

Is

Always **near!**

#26

To Be in Hell without an excuse

Is a sad tale **indeed**

Except to have lived among the holy flowers

And died away as **weeds**

To open your eyes

Amid the burning flames of unbelief . . . .

Appalled!

To have gone to church all of your life

Will be no excuse . . . . at **all!**

To be in hell without an excuse

You hate your brother **so**

Ignorant of the scriptures . . . . you Reap!

What you **sow**

It's no excuse

To die outside . . . . the Holy **gates**

For you never loved

And never gave . . . .

But for self . . . . To **take**

It's no excuse to live in vain

For a self-serving . . . . **lie!**

To plead . . . . for grace and mercy

While the weak and poor

Mourn . . . . and **cry!**

#25

There was a moment

And . . . .

An anonymous place

Our hidden secrets . . . .

But lonely days

Where our hearts and minds

Gentle touched

And established our love

That meant so much

An unspoken joy

We merely behold

Made us one!

Combined our souls

There was a moment

I can no longer find

The place we met

Where I called you mine!

#26

There are things . . . . That ought to be!

And **Should**

To go back in time . . . . And share my love!

I wish I **Could!**

There are many things . . . . I wish I could **do**

To go back . . . And tightly . . . . hold on

My enduring love . . . . for **you**

I wish I could have . . . . Cling

To just . . . . one more **day!**

Before you left . . . .

And took my heart **Away**

I wish I could

Roll back . . . .

The hands of **Time**

When we were one . . . . And you were **Mine!**

I wish I could . . . . I wish I **knew!**

How to recapture . . . . Your joy!

And my love . . . . for **You**

I wish I could . . . . bring you back!

Bring you closer! . . . . To bring you **near**

Into my heart . . . . Without dread

Or Fear**!**

I wish . . . . I could!

#27

The Open Door

It's not an invitation . . . . Although

It may seems

It's where one goes to find one's dreams

In a world . . . .

One cannot see

It's far beyond life and one's reality

Only the spiritual minded can enjoy or taste

While the wicked outside . . . .

Lay in waste

This Open Door

Is narrow, simple and low

Where the meek and the modest always go

It's not for those . . . . Who

Treacherously comes near

Full of deception and ungodly fear

The Open Door . . . .

Is closed!

To the self-righteous . . . .

And those . . . .

Whose lives . . . . are vain

Betrayed family and friends

For selfish and gluttonous gains!

#28

Jim Crow: A Cosmic Divide

She lived . . . .

On the other side

Of the fence

Actually though,

It was no barrier at all

But a demarcation

An

Embodied!

Of time, fate and bigotry

I can't go back

I can't return!

To a time . . . . My heart

Agonizingly searched

And prayerfully . . . . Yearned!

She can't come close

I can't come . . . . near

Her! . . . .

I long desire

But . . . .

Dreadfully fear!

#29

<u>Caring</u>

Compassion must be internalizes

So that mercy and goodness

Can actualizes

It is a force

That brings forth life

and removes

all fear, greed

and strife

It is a spirit that energizes . . . .

and speaks a language

Through caring eyes

It carriers no bitterness, grudges

       or guile.

Always giving, _____ always sharing

With a smile

It comforts and encourages

Until the very end . . . .

It's far sweeter,

than a close friend

      Caring!

    #30

In that final and dreadful day,

God will look over his beautiful world

And say

Where is my fruit from you?

A brilliant reply will not do

Many will ask . . . .

And not just some

With all bewilderment . . . . Will be undone!

Your talents, gifts and pleasurable years

All will be vanity . . . . and full of tears

After a life of waste and wicked fun

The question will be

What have you done?

Without excuses . . . . and nothing to say

At that fearful and terrible day

What will you do!

After living and parting . . . . your life away

What have you given?

What have you left?

Except for greed and loving yourself

Not your brother's keeper . . . . you will scorn

Through your pain and suffering . . . . you haven't learned

The eternally fire . . . . You will burn!

#31

Living this nightmare

No place to flee

No way out . . . . to fully love

Or fully be!

A life of joy and liberty

This society-like . . . . caste

Is a place where fear and ignorance

Perpetually . . . . last

One might awake and promptly realize

Its' a world of fantasy . . . . Constructed with lies

To keep one bound . . . . As mindless souls

And accept love for hatred . . . . as life unfolds

Freedom is not a place . . . .

But deep within the mind

Where few ever search

Or ever sought to find

One must be reborn . . . . To truly see

Its only . . . . when you love

You can . . . . authentically Be!

You will never truly age

Or ever grow old

Filled with love . . . .

An eternal soul!

#32

The grass is green, the sky is blue

It's my love that was made for you

The moon is full . . . . the sun is bright

It's your love that gives me light

The rain is wet . . . .

The snow is white

It's your love that makes life right

The summer is hot . . . . the winter cold

We have a love!

That can't be sold . . . .

Some people laugh and some sigh

But . . . . it is our love they cannot buy!

The day is gone . . . . the night is spent

We have a love

God sent!

The earth will spin . . . . Night into day

Yet, it is our love that will always stay

The grass is green . . . . the sky is blue

My love . . . . my joy is nothing . . . . without you

For my heart . . . . and my love

I give to you!

The grass is green . . . . The sky is blue

#33

If I had wings,

If I had White wings

I would fly above Jim Crow

But since I got no wings

And no White wings!

I'll just . . . .

Go on walking

Just as Black!

Just as proud

And Just as lonely . . . .

As before . . . .

#34

Do You Want Piece of My Love?

Do you want a piece of my love?

Like a half bake pie?

To hold and squeeze for a while

Then say good-by

Do you want . . . .

A piece of my love?

Until half past ten,

Trying to hold on . . . .

But afraid to end!

Do you want a piece of my love?

While we are close and near

Trying to keep . . . . to hope but fear

Do you want . . . . a piece of my love

Now . . . .

And then?

Do you want a piece of my love

And still be friends?

Do you want a piece of my love

You longed to seek?

Or is it . . . . my love

You want to hold on! . . . . and keep?

Do you want a piece of my love

For another day?

To make love to me _____ Hoping I'll stay!

Do you want . . . .

A piece of my love!

Do you want a piece of my love?

Cause . . . .

I'll be gone and you are left all alone

Do you want . . . . a piece of my love

To kiss _____ to come close

And hug?

Do you want a piece of my love?

#35

The difference between success and defeat

Is one . . . more . . . . try!

Proving . . . .

That failure . . . .

Is . . . . a contemptuous lie!

It's not intelligence . . . . It's the late midnight oil

Filled with doubts, regrets amid fears,

Sweat and toil!

Except . . . . for those who refused to see

To take hold of their freedom . . . . and true reality!

Success . . . . Is dissatisfied . . . . with the status quo

An endlessly quest . . . . Demanding more

The difference between . . . . failure and success

One does . . . . nothing

The other . . . . His best!

Repeatedly . . . . defeat accept unsupportable lies

Forcing the fearful to run and hide.

Success is a lonely and narrow trail . . . .

Without an end!

Thus . . . . choose competently . . . . your closest friends!

Success . . . . is a vision for one to see!

If one . . . . dare's to dream . . . .

Of what one can to be!

#36

A charming and pleasant smile

Is like a budding rose

Or a very lovely flower . . . .

A person who privately and steadily grows

Inwardly and painfully sours

Brings misery and grief . . . .

At his last dying hour!

Accordingly,

Happiness is a learned experience

Of growth, love and life

While misery is a predisposition

Of envy, hatred and strife!

One must learn to kindly give

Before he can learn to love

And laugh and live!

#36

When you have cried all night

And in the morning you weep!

Remember . . . .

The word of the Lord

Is a lamp to your feet!

When the world says . . . .

You won't and . . . .

Of course, you can't

Keep hope alive!

And . . . .

Don't you faint!

When others walk by the noon day light

You walk by faith!

And . . . . not by sight

When your troubles are stronger than you

And the answer comes too late

Remember, ...

God, always

Make . . . . the crooked ways straight

If you find yourself . . . .

In the valley of dry bones . . . . wait on the Lord,

And sit still

Don't act like . . . . mere men

Who live and die in their sins!

But as new creatures in Christ

Who are born again!

Our life is nothing but a mere test

For the wicked do all they can

And do their best

To get us off track

And stare hell in the face

To find ourselves in that hellish place

But we are kept . . . . we are preserved

Until the end!

By our Lord and Savior,

Jesus Christ . . . . Our Friend!

#37

<u>I can't show you my love!</u>

I can't show . . . . my love . . . . to you

I can't show you . . . . my love,

Like I do!

We don't belong . . . .

I don't belongs . . . . to you

I can't show you my love . . . .

In such a way

And yet . . . .

I want love . . . . and longed . . . . to stay!

I can't show you my love . . . .

Each time . . . . I hold you tight!

Cause . . . . I'll stay . . . . and try to hold on

And fight!

I can't show you . . . . my love

I can't explain!

I am hopeless and weak

Every time I make love

And call your name!

I can't show you my . . . . my love

Not a smile . . . . not even a touch

Your charisma . . . . your loveliness

Are all too powerful . . . . and means so much!

I can't show you . . . . my love

Any more . . . . and no further

You must look for love . . . . and find another!

I can't show you . . . . my love

Any longer . . . . to you!

You must seek and discover love

With someone new!

I can't confirm . . . .

I can't demonstrate!

Our love was true . . . . our love was real!

But far . . . . too late!

And far . . . . too many years

It was our love that was true and very real!

We must leave . . . . our old hiding place

Where we shared . . . . so many hours

So much love! . . . .

And so many days!

We must return . . . .

When we first became friends

To live . . . . and laugh . . . . and just pretend!

With smiles on our faces and joy in our hearts,

As though our love . . . . never began

Cause . . . . I can't show you . . . . my love!

38

Passing my way

In a moment of time

Just by chance . . . . To call her mine!

Passing my way

Love came quietly . . . . only to give

A life of love . . . . to cherish . . . . and live!

Passing my way

Love came

But surreptitiously . . . . walked on

Leaving to weep and to cry and moan

Your lovely smile . . . . is all I see

A life together . . . . Just you and me!

Passing my way

If just . . . . I only **knew!**

#39

How much happiness . . . . How much joy

And how much pleasure in loving **you!**

But now

I can only dream

And mournfully

Appreciate

A love that came

But Dreadfully . . . .

Late!

#40

Back then,

Our mothers . . . . called on God

A great deal more

When I was growing up

I think . . . . **everyday**

But now,

It's the all mighty dollar

That has its **sway**

Back then . . . .

Our mothers

Lived between two worlds

They lived . . . .

Between heaven and earth

Between racism and seeking God's **face**

Between love and hateful **ways**

Between their laughter and lonely **tears**

Counting the cost

In lives and agonizing **years**

Between their hopes and psychological **pain**

Dying and suffering in Jesus's **name!**

They looked for the promise

Yet to **be!**

But faith moved them

To stand and **see!**

Our mothers . . . . back **then**

Called on God,

As a child to his **friend**

When I was growing up

The more mothers prayed,

The worst life **got**

But God,

In his mercy . . . . knew their **lot!**

Oh! . . . .

Our mothers were filled with joy and plenty of **fun**

But God wasn't finished . . . . He wasn't **done!**

They remembered the crossing of the Jordon

And Red **Sea**

They remembered . . . .

How Jesus died on that **tree!**

They remembered

How He wiped away their **tears**

And rose **again**

And put away their past,

And all their **sins!**

Sometimes though,

We hear our mothers'**groans**

And sometimes **cry!**

But never forget

They are the promise

From the Most **High!**

#41

I am in a world

All of my own

It's a place

I don't belong!

I have this yearning . . . . deep within my mind

Where I pretend . . . . I am yours

And you are mine!

It's a world only I know

When I am lonely . . . . I often go

Where your warmth is greatly return

I no longer anguish, weep or yearn!

In my world . . . . I am filled with delight

As your love . . . . make things right

Although . . . .

I am in a dream . . . . All of my own

I am joyful . . . . loved

And free

While your caring love . . . .

Embraces me!

#42

An

Out . . . . of body

Experience

Whenever . . . . you are near

It's your kindness

It's your compassion

I . . . . Yearned

But fear!

I am . . . . enticed

To a higher plain

Each . . . . and every time

I see your face

Or call your name

And when my feelings . . . .

Begin to show

I calmly sigh

And silently . . . . go

That's the time!

I know . . . . you are real

These are the moments!

I truly feel

#43

There are many things

I've longed to say

And . . . . perhaps

I would

There are many times

I've yearned to embrace

And maybe . . . .

I should

There are many . . . . Sleepless nights

I wish!

I could . . . .

#44

One summer night

Her huge and spacious **grin**

She became my lover

And my precious **friend**

Nothing was said . . . . or ever **told**

She gave me her heart

But captured my **soul**

And now my life . . . .

is upside **down**

I am a weak little man . . . .

Or a sad looking **clown**

At this moment . . . .

I can't let **go!**

The love I had

And so much **more!**

That summer night

Her lovely **face**

Changed my life

And self-centered **ways**

My only request . . . .

To behold **again**

Her enchanting smile

And my precious friend

#45

As small as you are

As small as you are,

While should I be afraid,

As small as you are,

Why should I dread?

Except, _____

The fear of losing _____

The fear of losing

As small _____

As you are!

#46

I should be

I should be _____

I should be depress _____ and all deflated,

I am just lonely

And all frustrated

I should be,

I should be sad and filled with the blues

But, I can't' do nothing

But live and lose.

I should be _____

I should be glad,

I should glad she's gone!

I should be happy and not alone.

She came and she went _____

Maybe

She was heavenly sent!

So,

I'll just go on living and forget my love

And look for kindness _____ far above

I should be,

I should go on living and forget my lost,

I should go on _____ at any cost.

I should be.

#47

No one loves . . . .

A genius child

Don't know . . . . the reasons why

No one loves . . . .

A genius child

Who overcame repression and loathsome smiles

He gave to the needy and comforted the poor

From his heart . . . . always more

No one loves . . . .

A genius child

Though, ...

His heart always gives

Persuading others . . . . to truly feel!

No one loves . . . .

A genius child

Many are enslaved

Prisoners . . . . of their mind

Full of fear!

That strongly binds

No one loves . . . .

A genius child

Who have set . . . . many free

From their prejudices . . . . and misery

No one loves . . . . a genius child.

#48

I've treasured . . . .

Your love

When you were **near**

And cherished

Moment by moment

When you were **here**

I have held on . . . .

Hour . . . . by . . . . **hour**

And all the while

Enjoyed . . . . your love

And attractive . . . . s**mile**

I have valued our years

And . . . .

Unforgettable **days!**

Your compassionated . . . . look

And beautiful **ways**

I . . . . Can never discount

Nor . . . . ever . . . . **erase!**

I can't go back

Never . . . . to . . . . relive

A love I lost

But . . . .

so very real!

#49

I often long . . . . For the days

Swiftly . . . . Gone by

When we laughed and played . . . . without goodbyes

Since we were close . . . . and very dear

We were lovers . . . . so enchantingly near

I often long . . . . for the days

And the years . . . . Forever gone

A miserable little man . . . . so all alone!

Wishing for the days . . . . That can't return

My heart and soul . . . . Forever yearn!

At times . . . . though

My memories of sad goodbyes

Cause me to laugh . . .

Yet . . . . Weep!

And moan and cry!

#50

I just want . . . . To let you know

If I had your love . . . . I wouldn't let **go!**

I am reserve . . . . But truly must **say**

Your beautiful love . . . . has come my **way**

I would be pleased . . . . If I only **knew**

What dreams of mine . . . . Will actually come **true**

I just want . . . . To let you know

It's your loveliness

I strongly desire . . . . **More** and **More!**

Your lovely smile . . . . Is a budding **seed**

Promising me love . . . . and all I **need!**

I just want . . . . To let you know

It's your laughter

That's captured me **So!**

And now . . . . my days

Will . . . . ever be **spent**

Wishing . . . . you were mine

And . . . . **<u>Heavenly sent!</u>**

So . . . . In my thoughts

Night . . . . and **day**

It's what my heart **. . . .** has to **say!**

#51

<u>I have known love</u>

I have known love

As vivid as the open sky

                And

As wide as the ocean blue

Although, you said good-by

I am still in love with you!

I have known love . . . .

I have known love . . . . For many years

And many sleepless nights . . . . With crying and tears

I have known love . . . . for countless days

With fervent love . . . . in many ways

I recognized love . . . .

When I first met you

But I thought,

You would love me too!

I have known love!

I have known love . . . . much more

Than I can say

And hoped you . . . .

Would love me

The same . . . .

Exalted way!

I have known love!

#52

I don't seek affluence . . . .

Or self-seeking goals

Or myself . . . . to make a name

It's just your love

I seek to hold

I don't seek the highest mountain

Nor the Hall of Fame

It's just your love

When I call your name \

I don't seek glory in what I do

Just your smile

And a look from you

I don't seek praise

In what I say

Just your love . . . . in every way

I don't seek money

Nor things of greed

For your love

Is all I need

#53

I never knew

What love . . . . your beguiling love

Could make me see

I never knew love . . . . or a clear blue sky

Before I met you . . . . I wondered why?

I never knew

How to be myself . . . . and to stand very tall

You gave me your love . . . . you gave me all!

I never knew

What was artificial . . . . and what was real

You showed me your love . . . . you made me feel

I never knew

What love could be . . . . and what love could do

Until . . . . I gave my heart and love to you

You loved me . . . . As only you **can!**

My heart came alive . . . . and beat **again**

I never knew

That kind of love!

That was born on earth . . . . But came from **above!**

And thus . . . . I truly know

It's your love . . . . I'll never let go!

#54

I am pulled . . . .

Enticingly!

By your love . . . .

As . . . . g.r.a.v.i.t.y

Your lovely smile and stunning charm

Pull me closer

Each time . . . .

I fall into your arms

Like a puppet made of clay

Without a voice . . . .

And

Nothing . . . . to say!

Pulling me along . . . .

Like a puppet on a string

Or a feeble little man

Or a wretched little thing!

Your lovely face . . . .

Is all I see . . . .

Full of illusions . . . .

Enticingly!

#55

<u>How To Lift A Heart</u>

A handshake or a smile

Will sometimes **do**

Or . . . . a thought

Or a gift . . . . that says

Thank **you!**

To lift a heart . . . .

Is to save a **soul**

From distress, grief

And emotional **toil!**

To lift a heart means . . . .

To inspire

A poor lonely soul

To go further . . . .

And **higher**

To lift a heart . . . .

Is a gift from **above**

Filled with joy . . . .

And happiness . . . . And **love!**

#56

Have you ever walked away?

Have you ever walked away . . . . from love?

Have you ever walked away?

But deep in your heart . . . . You wanted to stay?

Have you ever walked away . . . . from love?

Have you ever had a song?

Have you ever song . . . . The **Blues**?

Have you ever cried the **Blues . . . .** All though the night

To turned and **Tossed**

To Dream of love . . . . you seized

But **lost?**

Have you ever . . . . song the **Blues**

And been down . . . . Lonely . . . . And low?

Until one day . . . . your smile

Your lovely face . . . . all glow?

Have you ever had a song . . . . Deep within your Heart?

A love you delightfully . . . . but sadly

Reminisce

A love you lost . . . . and deeply **Miss?**

#57

Fearfulness . . . .

Prevents you

From being yourself and glow

Shyness . . . .

From twisting

And twirling and letting yourself go

Afraid!

People may see . . . . your disappointments

Your hurt or pain

For their pleasure, greed or gain!

Like a prisoner . . . . locked into your mind

74

Unable to love . . . . or be loved . . . . or find!

You hope . . . . one day

That you may see!

How you can love . . . . and be love

And free!

To bring a smile to your face

To love and be loved

All your days

I'll wipe away . . . .

All of your tears

And give you love

Instead of pain, anger . . . . and fears!

My streets are dirty!

The air is polluted

The water is toxic

The soil is tainted

      And

You call me Dirty!

My community

Perfidious

My residence

Inhabitable

My family

Victimized

You call me Dirty!

Black leaders

Incompetent

Your elections

A fraud

My character denounced

    And

You call me dirty!

My humanity

Rejected

My dignity

Forbidden

Your pious

A sham

      and

You call me dirty!

My teachers

Ineffectual

Your educational system

Inadequate

Your school buildings

appalling

You call me dirty!

Your justice system

A mockery

Your policemen

Sadistic!

Your jails are filthy

Your prisons . . . .

Oppressive

      And

You call me . . . .

Violent!

Narratives

Plastic People

They are little more than androids, because arguably, they have flesh and bones, at the same time however, they are emotionally hollow and intellectual oblivious to their plight; also many of them are mentally wretched and are incapable in thinking for themselves. Countless of them are also neglectful, thoughtless, inconsiderate, and unpleasant to work with or around and besides uncaring, self-centered, self-seeking, self-interested, and narcissistic. And besides all of this, they are also rude and discourteous and are willing and enthusiastic to relinquish and exchange whatever authentic desires and feelings that they made have had and especially since their childhood in order to live as a nonentity. Now they are just mere objects who are no longer part of humanity; and thus have enslaved and confined themselves within a world of their own making.

Thus, they have become trapped and bound to a false reality and worldview. At the same time though, they are kept and encircled with illusions of freedom and liberty that they believe they enjoy. They dislike anyone who do not think like them and especially those who are free and has developed into full human beings.

Church services are often filled with Plastic people, with plastic sermons, plastics prayers and plastic blessings. And besides all of this, politicians are often very plastic people and will often cry at funeral services and wretchedly, likewise, a number of preachers will repeatedly follow collaboratively. Let's not forget though, that there are many mindless and plastic parents who are raising their plastic children to become precisely plastic, but many of these plastic children leave home before their life become as completely lifeless and as meaningless and lead plastic lives. Generally, many marriages are plastics; wives are plastic and so too are many husbands. Plastic people however, do not belong to any racial or cultural group and cannot be defined as Black, White or Brown; they are just plastic. Most of them are incapable of providing affections or friendship because they have never known love since they are only plastic people themselves.

While plastic people have many different customs and practices, they all have been molded, formed and or fabricated as youths to become plastics individuals instead developing into fully formed individuals. Many of them have no understanding that the world does not revolved around their obsession and fixation and consequently they nourish themselves on the fear, intimidation, terrorism and coercion. When threats are no longer effective they seek to pull others down who do not believe or act as they. Moreover, some of them will often speak about how much money they have expensive homes, cars and other toys that they have accumulated and also to show that it is better to be plastic person than a full formed human being.

While their hearts are dark, they despised other who does not view them as exceptional, unique, and extraordinary and especially above the common people. The term plastic is a metaphor for neurosis because these people are unable to form any healthy and intimate relationships. At the same time, a few of them would like to escape this living psychological torture but at the same time, they are gratified in just tearing real people down by destroying characters and besides they are too afraid of the real and outside world. And besides, they know nothing about the meaning of respect, kindness and self responsibly and thus see no wrong in themselves, but only in others who are not like them, plastic Furthermore, the world must revolve around them at all times but sometimes though; they appear to show some form of normalcy just to impress and manipulate others so that they will not be exposed as plastic people and also to conceal their madness and insanity and thus, to gain popularity and social status.

One of the reasons why Jim Crow Laws were so powerful and entrenched into mainstream society was to provide some sense of comfort and emotional security to plastic people and allowed them to live in a false reality and a make-believe world. Back then, even Black middle class people enclosed themselves in various enclaves to protect their sense of self as plastic people. Today, Black intellectuals are not exempt from becoming plastic individuals; lower class Black people also seem to love plastic credit cards and real debt without obligations. What these plastic people have in common is that they enjoy finding fault with others in order to make themselves feel that they are better than and more outstandingly and thus they feel loftier.

It is very difficult if not impossible for anyone to live with these plastic people who are filled with resentment, bitterness, jealousy. Like credit cards, these people like everything plastic and even their false smiles are plastic; and when they die, they will be buried in a plastic coffin and find themselves in "Hell" with nothing but plastic people who will see them for who they actually are, devils!

Returned to Sender

The people who used to live here do not live here anymore; maybe they were very important people and very well known. They got a letter the other day from a U.S. Congressman, stamped "returned to sender". I never got a letter from my congressman though. He never was underfed, underpaid, or undernourished and he never lived in my neighborhood, never drank in my bar, stood in unemployment lines or stood at the welfare window. Just the same though, I decided to write my congressman. I told him all of the problems that I have had in this here world that it is a wonder that I am still alive. I also told him the many ways that he might help me. Initially, I asked him if he could help me find my ex-wife Deloris, who ran away more than ten years ago taking our eight children. Furthermore, I asked him if he could help me get a job and if not, help me get my disability checks. After weeks of waiting for my congressman's assistance, he finally his responded, "returned to sender".

Depravity

Today, for many African-Americans, self-delusion and self-indulgence have created a make-believe world of irresponsibility. Even God, Heaven and angels have been redefined and recreated to fit this illusionary world. With the assistance of several entities, global television, T.V evangelicalism, the public educational system and together with Black leadership have not only made this "New World Order" possible but highly profitable for a few. It seems that each group specializes in selling dreams to certain classes of people and thus false dreams and false hopes. These dreams are nothing new and yet they are still powerful and very attractive to the wayward in order to lead them to an everlastingly pit.

Moreover, what is so distressing is that many of our Black preachers are little more than gatekeepers standing in the doorway of hell with sincere smiles and supposedly with love in their hearts to welcome the blind, the faithless and the self-righteous. Every day the blind is leading the blind but soon many of their followers will discover that their leaders are mere wolves in sheep clothes and unprofitable servants. At the moment though, it appears that there is no way out of this dilemma and no hope for the weak, the ignorant and the lost. I believe however that a "change will come" but not without disillusionment, hardships and a sense of hopelessness.

Black families of the Post-Civil Rights Era, and especially those families who were born after 1950 having enjoyed relative prosperity all their lives, believe there could be no difficulties, trouble, or tragedy to whatever decision they made. Traditional religious values were gradually removed from family life, if not totally ignored or neglected. Thus, Black parents unwittingly instilled in their children a world-view of selfishness and treachery; and in their effort to prevent their children from having to suffer lack or necessities or to encounter the horrors of Jim Crow, they overly nurtured, protected and shield them from the real world of hard work, racism and bigotry. The saying "Lift As You Climb" has lost its religious and spiritual meaningfulness which include self-reliance, self-determination, family unity and the importance of hard work.

Consequently, countless of Black children were not emotionally prepared to enter the real world of difficulties, hardships, failures or racial discrimination; and now many black children are like a wondering stars without direction or guidance. Too many of them have lost hope for a better tomorrow. Their dreams are all gone now and they no longer dreams, dreams of greatness and protectors within their community, instead many have become outlaws, gangsters and predators within their own family and community. A new reality has now emerged and it is one of neurosis and psychosis that have become the 21st century plague, a spiritual disease, a mindless entity and demonic.

This condition cannot be removed by sit-ins, freedom-marchers or Freedom Riders, nor can speeches or civil demonstrations heal this sickness. We must go back to our old-time religion when humility was normalcy and a life-world of togetherness instead of old wives tales and folk-lore; a time when laughter and joyousness overcame hatred and envy, a time when honesty and trust were close friends instead of abstract and empty words, covered with deceit and ungodly rebelliousness, disobedience and defiance. But that is all gone now! Back then, we were Black people, real Black people!

The Old Railroad Tracks

It has been almost 50 years ago since I left this small town; I supposed I am one of a few individuals who was born here ever came back to visit. About a mile away and across the railroad tracts, in the midst of a wooded area was my neighborhood; it was a refuge, a place of encouragement, compassionate and kindness. Yet I was nostalgic, reflective and longing to return to a life world of caring, trust and assurance. Probably a voice called me back, a voice without a sound or words to be heard. Perhaps I came back for my soul or that part of me that I left behind, or lost, that part of me that cherished a smile or a gentle touch, that part of me that valued friendship, churchgoing and family gathering or that part of me that instilled a sense of belonging and a sense of the Here and Now". But that is all gone now; yet and still, I believed I can still hear the laughter of children playing and old men telling the same old jokes.

But I was home, it was safe for us back then; we were far away from outsiders, not in terms of distance but an unknown life-world that was only discernible to the spiritual enclave. As I stood on the old railroad tracts, disturbed and jumbled memories hurriedly through my mind as though they were carrying me back through time. These mental pictures permitted me to revive, experience, capture and re-capture a forgotten world of longed ago, a world of want but full of dreams, a world of terror but full of hope, a world of oppression but full of longed suffering and a world painful memories, but full of joy, a world—fearful of outsiders and strangers, but yet closeness of family.

Suddenly I no longer saw the rusty old railroad tracts, but recently laid steel waiting for the next train to cross its path. The grass was now greener, the sky bluer and the dried up old lake besides the railroad tracts were now full of fresh water and overflowing with fish. I was home. Toxic air was no longer a distance memory now; I could recall the poisonous odor, the sickening air and the foul atmosphere. Back then though, citizens always showed signs of death on their faces and a sense of despondency. The old creeks and streams near the railroad tracks were also toxic. People got sick and died. The dying always called a preacher while on their death bed to ask for pray. The birds did not die though; they just flew away, like I and so many others before me, took to the corroded railroad tracts, the path to an unknown world. We were escaping a world of illusion, an imaginary world of contented deception.

Those railroad tracks and the bridge where I was standing reminded me that freedom, true freedom achieve not by ignoring cruelty but by facing oppression and internal fears. At the same time though, I was aware that there was something beyond myself, beyond the old railroad tracks, beyond the polluted environment and suspicious mind-sets that were filled with hatred, debauchery and abomination. The Black church in my community that was on the colored side of the railroad tracts encouraged me to survive and endure. No one talked about equal rights or due process, back then; we were concern with living with optimism and anticipation knowing that one day the crooked road would be made straight. At one point in my life I did not believe that I would live to see that day. On my way to school, I got my foot caught between the railroad tracks. I attempted to remove my foot with the greatest effort but to no avail. The train was rapidly moving towards me, and suddenly, someone pulled me away from those tracts.

I never did see who pulled me away from those tracts but I was convinced it was my guardian angel. I used to cross those railroad tracts every day as I walked to the catholic school where those old White nuns used to greet me daily with their prayerful smiles and heavy hand. As I think back now, I supposed their prays and punishment saved my life; perhaps they are in heaven now wondering if their firm, unyielding and demanding love did any good.

Roller-Skates and Pancakes

In my neighborhood when I was growing up during the 1940's and the 1950's, roller-skates were fashionable during Christmas season. Many groups of young African American boys and girls could be seen and heard rushing through various sections of town from early morning to early afternoon. Our ages ranged from 9-16 years of age and each of us was loaded up with a variety of fruits that would last us all-day. Christmas for us, was a time of liveliness in which we shared each other's companionship rather than personal gifts, toys or indoor games. We skated to a number of astonishing places. The places we visited were always quite surprising because we rarely went outside of our recognized cultural boundaries.

Those boundaries were imaginary and invisible "White" lines; but once we passed the next traffic light, crossed the railroad tracks and turned the corner, we were home. We were safe, back then. We sensed a peaceful spirit that seemed to engulf our souls the moment we crossed that indiscernible line within our Black community. By and large though, we seldom passed through up-scale White communities, but Christmas season was special. During this holiday season we regularly skated through up-scale White communities. Back then, though it was relative safe for us because it was Christmas time and besides, we skated with urgency. To us, back then, those up-scale White neighborhoods were incredible beautiful places to visit; our awareness of such life-style encouraged many of us to dream of a better day, a better time, a better place and better opportunities.

Back then, when I was growing up, we used to cross those invisible lines daily as we left our neighborhood, our life-world of certainty and entered a strange new world of uncertainty. I supposed things are very different now; there are no visible lines of demarcation and no billboard signs that counseled you not to enter a certain district or neighborhood or signs that determined one's place in society. Nowadays however, our advanced communities are simple an illusionary world of a deceptive performance and a mockery of authenticity of a lived experience of togetherness and closeness. In our neighborhood back then, kindness and thoughtfulness were atmospheric; we took faithfulness and friendship and unlocked doors for granted.

A number of us however, internalized those images of manicured lawns and majestic homes that became a metaphor for self-determination. For most of us though, those images became a dream deferred. Years later though, a few of us accomplished that dream but not without an exchange. Some of us exchanged a moral life with the Back community for debauchery and treachery. A number of us and especially Black leadership, back then, exchanged substandard housing and overt oppression for another form of oppression that was more shameful and illusory. Many of us erroneously accepted economic and political advancement, racial integration and the illusionary "American Dream", food-stamps, section-eight housings, Free or Reduced School Lunch Programs and high unemployment and irresponsible living.

Others, however, traded a life-world of self-assurance within the Black community for suspicion and a powerful religious conviction for apprehension. Many of use replaced self-confidence for cynicism and self-determination for inner-anger. Nowadays, and for all of our advancements we are a more isolated, fearful people who psychologically lost. A few of us though often yearn for that forgotten world of cultural and racial boundaries; it was a place where kindness, laughter and affection dwelled.

Nevertheless, before our final voyage within the up-scale White communities in which we journeyed, a number of us had pancakes for breakfast, but not the kind we consume today. Our pancakes were authentic;

they were simple but rich with natural ingredients; it was down-home cooking and prepared with real buttermilk. There was nothing artificial about our mealtimes. No one it seems can reproduce that kind of cuisine that nurtured our bodies and lifted our spirits. Most boys I knew played with lizards but not during Christmas time. Back then, it was time for roller-skates and pancakes.

Why Black People Hate Each Other

Introduction

Why is there so much killing, stealing, robbery, burglary, assault within the Black community? What is the solution? There is no clear answer to this daunting and complex problem. Not all Black people hate each other but within the Black community, there seems to be much hatred.

I have regularly and almost daily experienced as well as many other successful and well educated Black men the open hostility, bitterness and resentment from many Black men who are not as successful and or as well educated. Often though, these inferior minded Black men's vindictiveness, malice, is often well hidden until they find an opportunity to bring down others to their level of inferiority. Typically, these Black men are heartless individuals who find pleasure in seeing others below them. Continuously, they are not only annoyed, distraught, distressed but are emotionally and mentally troubled when they see others receiving recognition, acknowledgment and or applause.

Incessantly, these inferior minded Black men seem to hunger and thirst for the demise of others. This mindset is a form of madness and disrespect for all who have achieve goals in life.

Worldviews

There are two worldviews within the Black community that is contrary and contradictory. In one worldview, Black people see this country as a land of opportunity if you work hard; the other worldview see the world from the standpoint of getting all you can from others, no matter what the personal or social cost. This attitude is conceived from envy, and a craving and a deep-seated covetousness mentality that creates a psychological need to be someone other than themselves. It is an inward hatred that leads to an inner misery and need to blame others for their plight.

However, successful and well educated Black men must live in two worlds; the world that they were born into and full of acceptance but now not recognizable. They are well aware that they are no longer welcome and accepted within the Black community, but are seen as outsiders and strangers. For many, the other world is a place that is psychologically, intellectually and passionately comfortable; at the same time though, there seems to be a sense of disillusionment. It is a place, and a world where many of these men are perceived as Black and not as an individual. Those who experienced Jim Crow seem to adapt rapidly to their successful life style because they have been taught to bend, modify and to regulate their behavior.

It is a behavior that many fruitless and unproductive Black men have failed to accept and or recognize, thus, conflict arise within countless of Black families as well as within the Black community. Not only has this fact prevailed, but also there several fictitious and illusory racial lines of demarcation with in the Black community. For example, there are **Blacks, Browns, Yellow, high-yellow, half White s and ¼ Whites**. During the 1940' and the 1950's, these illusory racial groups were very pronounced in their attitudes, beliefs, organizations, church and social affiliations. It seems that during those times, the closer a person was toward being White one's social privilege s and status.

Thus, in order to maintain one's social privilege, opportunities and self-determination it was essential to repudiate, disclaim, and or reject one's true identity and or any closeness to Blackness. This caused many of these various groups to create distinctions among themselves. No one desire d to be Black during those times and others even hated themselves, but those groups who were on a higher social scale did not mind their lot as long as they were not on the bottom of the social ladder. Many members of these groups married within their own social and racial boundaries so that they would not be contaminated with Blackness. Be White as much as you can, but by all means deny any hit of Blackness.

In recent years though, a number of questions have been asked as to who is truly Black, but no one has illuminated as to what the term Black and or Blackness really mean.

What's Wrong with Black Women?

Well, _____ for one thing, they watch too much television and are influenced by countless of White men buying their wives, girlfriends and mistress new cars, fur coats and very expensive homes. There were no new cars in my neighborhood when I was growing up except the new police cars that I rode in when I got arrested. Back then, I saw a fur coat once when I was washing windows at a downtown store as White women were passing by. Back then, Black men were not even allowed to buy very expensive homes and if they did, they were considered troublemakers and menaces to the social order and moreover uppity. Their achievement told White people that they were equals or even better than most White people. I have seen numerous of very expensive homes while I was doing yard working for rich White people.

Today, Black women crave to have what White women have had for years and have also taken for granted. Furthermore, many Black women desire "Bling-Bling" to reflect a degree of self-importance and are completely unaware that many White women are seeking to be like natural Black women and no amount of material possessing can transform them into what they are not and can never become. But some Black women believe that expensive jewelry can compensate for their feelings of insignificance and thus, crave diamond rings. I did not see diamond rings when I was growing up, but I did see a few diamond rings on televisions back then. Those diamond rings were far out of my price range; I never did see one for under twenty-five dollars.

Soon after, I decided that I did not want any television sets in my home; it caused too much trouble between my wife and me. After one hour of my wife watching television I was weeks in the hole and could hardly pay monthly rent and besides our water bill was already two months past due. Television got me broke ever since "Superman" and "Spiderman" went off the air. However, many Black women don't mind being broke so long as they look attractive, lovely and sexy while no food is in the house. Black women like vacations too; I did go on a vacation once, it was years ago when I was sent Vietnam. Credit cards are also a Black woman's dream and besides they come in the mail free of charge, and just "sign on the bottom line" and they too can have everything White women have always enjoyed.

Clothes, Black women love clothes, they have a credit card for shoes, another for hats, another for self-expression and another for Sunday church. For some Black women though, deeply in debt appears to be a status symbol of arrival and progress and at the same time "Forgive Us of Our Debt" has been mistranslated. When I was growing up, I prayed for a real Black woman, but that too, has been misinterpreted. Back then, all most Black women really wanted was a real Black man, but nowadays though, all they seem to truthfully want is a sugar daddy. What is wrong with Black women today is that they seem to have substituted love for **things** and the **"authentic"** for **vanity.** There are no more "Five and Dime" stores any more, they are all gone now and besides, television has ruin my marriage and so many others since "Superman" and "Spiderman" went off the air.

Years ago, there were laughter, smiles, and joyfulness; back then, dating was holding hands while the old lady was observing through the torn and outdated curtains. It was a time when marriages was endorsed vie nods of several old church ladies. It was character and faith and not self-indulgence that decided one's destiny and a time when wisdom was like the early morning dew and the early spring showers. But that life-world and lived experience is forever gone and will never return. It was also a time with the natural eye that real Black women were commonplace but now spiritual discernment is almost necessary and required. **What's wrong with most Black women?** Perhaps, they have lost that **"loving feeling"** of being true to themselves, true to reality and true to their calling in becoming authentically beautiful, lovely and Black!

Paradoxical, a lovely and attractive smile often capture a Black man's heart and surely much more so than deceitful pretense. Unknowingly though, many Black women are not aware of their influence and supremacy over the Black man's emotions and ego. Unconsciously and unmistakably, Black men are forever fascinated, captivated and mesmerized by Black women's attractive words and are often compelled to embrace a world of compassion, gentleness and thoughtfulness. Black then, when I was growing up, mothers and grandmothers knew about this hidden wisdom of true self-acceptance and the high value of Black womanhood that has longed been forgotten by too many Black women.

Today, attentive grandmothers are no here, hiding behind the old dirty and broken window while silently peering through the torn and outdated curtains. It is the Black woman's heart, thoughts and mind that will permit her to dream and to hope for an authentic life of true love and self-actualization. I cannot truly tell anyone what's wrong with Black women, but I can advocate a solution _____ humility. It means to be strong without boasting, determine without masculine, self-confidence without pride and wisdom from beyond and within. Television should no longer be allowed to define, alter or revise the reality of Black womanhood. Primary, the news media's chief objective is to consistently distort the truth about Black women and to transport them into a world of make-believe and toward the shores of self-rejection, self-hatred, depression, and even suicide. Perhaps, television has cause many Black women to forsake the reality of their beautiful Blackness and to falsely cling to a fantasy and an illusionary world where Whiteness and White women are somehow and in some way superior.

What's wrong with Black women today is that they as individuals are totally unaware that they are more precious and are more valuable than all of the gold in the world; but many refuse to accept their rightful place in the world as queens, mothers and parents with a resolve, a calling and a purpose to achieved their highest goals and dreams. Back in Egypt, years

ago, a Black woman ruled not only her homeland but the whole entire

known world and without a word, if she lifted her left or right hand she

could determine the course of history. Life and death were within her fingers

and no one dared to question her right, privilege or request; her word was

absolute. Thus, these facts are not on television.

Street Lights

Back then, when I was growing up during the early 1950's there

were no street lights in my Colored neighborhood. It was always very dark

at sunset and so much so that no one could see their hands in front of their

face. As acquaintances past by their neighbors' houses they spoke politely to

the residents even though they did not see each other's faces and besides, the

residents knew their generational relatives. The Colored residents somehow

knew who were passing by their houses; perhaps, by the sound of voices

or by the shadowy figures from the reflection of the moon light. Speaking

caring to neighbors was an ordinary and expected lived experience and

particularly to older people. During the night, our neighborhood, deprived of

street lights became a blanket of darkness and yet, no one ever experienced

intimidation or danger.

There was no apprehension of being robbed, assaulted or beaten

in our neighborhood and besides, once we past the last traffic light and

crossed the rusty railroad tracks and entered the deteriorated Colored

section of town, we were all safe back then. During night time the sheer

blackness of our neighborhood would seem to be an unnerving, intimidating and a petrifying place for outsiders and certainly for White people. No White person ever dared to be seen in our neighborhood at night, except one time though. It was a time when a White man from up north came down to the South and questioned the fact that the White communities had street lights but not the Black communities. After a long legal battle our Black neighborhood was finally provided street lights, but no one in our community was really thrilled or delighted to have street lights installed at every corner.

Our Black neighborhood was no longer a place of privacy, discretion, secrecy and pleasure; we were no longer inaccessibility and quarantine from outsiders. It was very disappointing and mournfully for numerous of Colored people who lived there. For one thing many of the deacons could no longer go to old ladies' houses as soon as it got dark, stayed overnight and leave before just before daybreak. The Colored women, who owned moonshine houses had to take precautionary measures and many of them, became distrustful and observant about a few of their clients. It was also normal for those women to have Bibles on their coffee tables: and besides, many of them commonly pretended to be churchgoing, God loving and very prayerful persons during the day time.

A few Colored women had to be especially evasive about who they invited to their place of business because important Colored men like preachers, school teachers and Black civic leaders were regularly there. Therefore, certain places within the neighborhood became sort of a high society location where only a few choice individuals were allowed. Houses of prostitution as well as gamble houses were also a thriving business; even a few selected and well-known married White men such a lawyers, judges, and school district mangers. From time to time, a few White women visited

96

several houses to "let their hair down", they were no longer White women but ordinary and down-to-earth ladies who were there only to "have a good time". It was an interlude and a place to escape the prejudice and bigotry of the day; it was also a place of true freedom and especially an unknown space of sovereignty.

Once they entered, no one had an important title; they were all equal and recognized by their first names only and of course, they provided a great deal of trade before the street lights were placed in the Colored neighborhood; but now, they could no longer hide their new Cadillac's, Mercedes and BMW's and slip in the backdoors of their preferred places. Consequently, those street lights cost everyone a secret place to express themselves and to make money during the time of life-threatening Jim Crow Laws.

White men who were municipal and public leaders decided to replace the normal state required illumination with cheap, low-priced and cut-rate street lights. Back then, we were closed to the outside world where outsiders perceived our culture as uncanny and ghostly, but soon afterwards, it was known that paved streets were been placed in our community and with superior street lights. Those new street lights shattered a concealed and very deceptive and invisible life-word of pretending within the Black community. Countless of old Colored ladies could no longer pretend to be lowly, humble, submissive and weak and likewise, the Black men could no longer hide their faces in the depth darkness within their community. At the same time though, many of them had an untold and an unknown influence with some of the most powerful White men during that time. But that is all gone now, at least to the naïve.

Today, distinguished and recognized Black television preachers are playing a new game like the old Colored ladies back then who played the role of lowliness and compliance. The difference though, back then, you got what you paid for, as immoral as it was; but now, all you get is false dreams, deceitful lies and fraudulent promises that are designed to make them rich while corrupting and confusing the weak. Now though, I wish there were no renowned Black television ministers, paved roads or street lights!

Three Things White Women Hate

Not all White women hate, in fact, I believe that most are unable to truly hate, yet and still there are however so much inner fear for many of them. First, many White women hate to see Black men and White women together and especially personally, secondly, they hate to see White men and Black women together and especially showing affection for one another. But most of all, they hate to see their "Pure" White children playing together with half-White children and particularly in their enclosed and protected neighbors. For the most part though, these women's feelings of hatred did not come about because of some scientific knowledge, but were imparted, inculcated and infused by a world-view that whiteness is somehow much more grander. Unknowingly, though, they as children were nurtured, educated and encouraged to adhere to an attractive frame of reference of privilege, opportunity and whiteness.

To observe anything other than their false reality of racial supremacy created an absurdity and a phobia that somehow they are losing their "true" identity as distinctive and exceptional White individuals. However, their world-view that has never existed but hatred is the only way for many to deny reality in order to maintain some sense of self; and if hatred is not part of their innate temperament, then fear instinctively and spontaneously surface. Fear then, become a psychological defense mechanism from danger nevertheless, many White women somehow escape their illusionary world of make-believe and become free human beings full of joy and laugher. But the sad truth is that so many White women feel protected and safe within their sanctuary of whiteness and are threatened whenever they face an alternative worldview.

Hatred allows many White women a method of departure and a flight from realism and thus fear becomes a refuge and a sanctuary to guard against actuality. Understandable though, but unlike the old Negro slaves who were held captivate and oppressed against their will, for White women though, there are no chains on their feet or hands, no restrictions and no laws except a racist and antiquated social norm. This method maybe a more frightful process of upholding, reserving and keeping a fraudulent world-view. Many White women have been inculcated from early childhood to accept as factual a system that has kept them from growing mental, emotionally, economically and socially advancing to their highest potential. Thus, many White women have freely given themselves over to an oppressive system that has kept them in psychological chains, has provided false hopes and promises of a superior existence, as long as they live as psychological White slaves who believe they free.

Then, the White man is, of course pleased, because they can maintain Control of their White women and keep them from straying outside of their "pure White race'. Thereby, assuring White society that all of their White women are "safe from sexual attacks by Black men. Years ago, when

I was growing up Lynching was an overt message to the Black community that White women is the property of White men and that Black men would be taking their lives into their hands if they cross that illegal and prohibited racial line. Today, other subtly and craftily methods are used to keep Black and White women from developing intimate relationships. Nowadays, one sure method is to locked up as any Black men as possible and all within the law. However, other methods were gradually introduced into the mainstream as collective and accepted narratives.

These narratives are usually cloaked in various forms to include news articles, movies and educational programs in order to mislead, twist, falsify and exaggerate the life-world and lived experiences of Black men; thus, each generational of White women can be notified, informed and advised to stay away from Black men. These cautionary tales indoctrinate White women not only hate but fear all Black men for their own good. Therefore, most White women take comfort in this strange notion that they are somehow superior and special. In order to maintain their sense of manhood and White identity, White males must frequently lift the White woman up to the status of a goddess. If these narratives and world-view are eliminated, destroyed or removed from the psychic of White women, White males then lose all of their control, authority, self-esteem, self-importance and self-worth in their "whiteness".

Consequently, the Black man is a threat to the very existence of the White male's view of himself as a ruler and controller of all things and hence, the expression and worldview of "White supremacy" must continue its madness no matter how futile, hollow or hopeless it may seem. But for now, many more people mourn under this insanity and utter nightmare!

The Interview

Human Resource Officer: Good evening Mr. Richardson, why did you apply for this job?

Richardson: I applied for this job so that I can get involved in everybody's business. and drive them crazy!

HR: What is your goal?

Richa: to upset and trouble everyone who work with me!

HR: Why?

Richa: because I feel inferior, unsuccessful, inadequate, irrational and very angry with everyone.

HR: Well Mr. Richardson, I am very sorry, but we are not hiring crazy people at this time, however, we will be hiring a number of Black men within the next year, that is, if you are crazy enough.

Richa: Yes madam! I am very crazy! I have lied, defied, backstabbed and bad-mouthed my work leaders and even my Black supervisors.

HR; well, Mr. Richardson, you definitely sound crazy enough! But the job does not pay very much.

Richa: I do not care about the pay, just so long as I can cause misery, dissatisfaction, disgruntlement, grief, dissension, turmoil and disorder.

HR: You have proven to us that you are very crazy and we will be contacting you very soon to let you know that you have officially accepted the job offer.

Richa: Thank you very much for this opportunity to allow me stirrup malice, bitterness and resentment.

HR: If you are successful, you may be promoted to supervisor.

Richa: I do not want to be supervisor because that is too much responsibility, but I will Definitely tell the supervisor what to do, how to do his job and what I expect from other co-workers.

HR; Do not worry Mr. Richardson, we will not trouble you for that supervisor position, but as soon as you run off this supervisor by your undesirable, destructive, and harmful attitude, we will find another replacement who you can easily control and or castigate.

Richa: Thank you.

HR; oh, by the way, Mr. Richardson, do you know any crazy White women who may like to create hell for others?

Richa: No, I am not sure at this time, but I do know many crazy Black women, because I have been married seven times; and my last wife, Ella May ran off with our eight children and I have not seen them since.

HR; No Mr. Richardson, we have enough crazy Black women around here who are giving us hell everyday and besides, we do not need any more trouble with EEO. Yet and still, Mr. Richardson, we are seek one crazy White woman who are just as crazy or as insane you are.

Richa: I may know one crazy White woman though.

HR; When you find her please tell her to call HR if she has a very profound craving to create hell on earth.

Richa; I will do so.

HR; Goodbye.

The Outcast

It was in this small segregated and isolated sleepy Alabama town that the interstate bus came to a stop. A few minutes later, a strange middle-age Black woman gently stepped deliberately from the bus, but her truthful age betrayed her appearance. Her wrinkled face filled with cracks and ingrained lines that articulated her years of unspoken narratives of an empty life, a lived experience of emotional and psychological pain, disillusionments and dreams deferred. She took a cab to her great grandmother's home where she grew up as a young child and knocked and knocked several times but no one answered. Later, several small children came to the door but they were terrified and fearful to open the door to strangers and besides, they were taught that the KKK was a powerful and treacherous group.

Finally, the middle-age woman shouted her name and identified who she was. A short time later an old lady discerningly came to the door and discovered that the strange middle-age Black woman was her granddaughter who she had not seen in more than twenty years. Weeks later the middle-age woman made a enough emotional and physical improvement to go outside of her house to walk through the small segregated town remembering the time when she was young and innocent a with bright future. She also recalled the many opportunities, her dreadful failures and her wrongfulness. But she was home; it was beginning a new life, a new beginning and perhaps, a new hope; for her, it was a new day.

Unsuspectingly, though, after the old man's wife died several years ago he was looking for help as he overheard the strange middle-age Black woman looking for work. He thoughtfully and circumspectly asked her if she was willing to work for him. She agreed and over several months the woman became transformed in attractiveness, attitude, and charm with better clothing. Her youthfulness returned. Now she was home and welcome back into the local Black church, but many of the old-timers in that small town remembered her lifestyle and wasteful existence many years before she came back home town. Others wondered why the old man accepted her as a virtuous, shy and unassertive woman.

It was rumored that perhaps the old man had been fooled by her deception, treachery and charm. Yes it was true for years she had been a prostitute, homeless and jailed often, but the old man saw none of that. He saw a very pleasing and beautiful lady, full of love and joy and always smiling with laughter. For the old man though, no words or gossip could change that; for sure, his heart was fixed and appeared to have loved her with a desire that far exceeded mere physical affection. It was not his money that motivated her to be transformed; it was his heart and desires to please her. But she gave him much more than he could have dream of, a new beginning and a reason for being.

Not long after they were married; she was no longer an outcast or an ex-prostitute but the dream of his life. Nevertheless, the town's people continued to marvel their intimacy, liveliness and passion for living. At the same time the town's people could not understand nor could they appreciate the kind of joy and happiness that the old man and the middle-aged woman shared and relished. They were like a light that shines in darkness

The old maid

During the 1940's and the 1950's, Jim Crow was the law of the land. For Black people though, it was a time characterized by intimidations, persecutions, harassment, violence and cruelty. A time when Black people were not allowed to enter all White establishments such as rest rooms, public libraries hotels, motels rooms and White restaurants. Within the Black community however, it was a time of sharing, generosity and closeness. Consequently a number of African Americans constructed boarding house for their guests and visitors. They did not require business licenses from the local White city officials; they really didn't care as longed as they remained on their side of the railroad tracks. I recalled one middle-aged African American woman who owned a boarding house but over the years she received very few guests and visitors. A few older members within the Black community knew little about her and did not assume she was just an old spinster. Others assumed she disliked people in general because she did not socialize.

After all, the middle-aged women had been living alone for almost 30 years. One evening during a hot summer day a middle-age man saw the middle-aged woman working in her flower garden stopped to ask her about a room for rent. A short time later, the woman was seen talking to this strange middle-aged man, but within an hour or so, she was laughing and smiling as if she was a young girl again. For years the town's people daily passed her boarding house never really recognized her as part of their community and most of them never spoke or looked up to recognized her. Previously, they quietly passed her house as if she was as stranger or an outsider. A few wondered while others whispered as to what the woman could be so joyful about. Soon a crowd of watchers and listeners gathered across the street from the boarding house watched as she seemed to become alive with laughter or born again.

Later a number of the town's people came over to invite the man to their town and both of them to their local church. They did not dared inquire about what they had seen and heard, but now they were no longer apprehensive about the middle-age woman's sequestered behavior. In their eyes, the middle-aged woman was a different person as if a transformation had taken place in front of their face. For weeks they observed the middle-aged man and the woman coming to church together but speculated about their seemly close relationship and what was going on inside of the boarding house. No knew that the man left that small town more than 35 years ago and knew most of the older people there but they did not discern who he was or where he came from. Soon, they often observed the woman's fashionable new clothes and her majestic smiles.

Now, she was no longer the old maid, the stranger or the outsider within and yet many wondered what had happen and why such a sudden change in her behavior and lifestyle. Later, the local Black community regarded the couple to be very close friends or lovers as they were regularly seen having dinner at local Black restaurants. Moreover, and surprisingly, they were also seen sleeping out on the front poach of the boarding house with an enclosed screen. Many of the town's people who passed in front of her house during the night could hear both of them laughing while soft music was playing. What was even more strange and unsettling for the town's people, as was reported, the middle-aged woman and man were seen during the early morning hours singing and dancing together while working in the flower garden.

The middle-aged women now had a reason to smile and laugh after years of emotional pain and recluse. Her heartache, her feelings of dejection, her state of unhappiness and the impossibility of finding love and acceptance were slowly disappearing. Her restless nights were gone and or fading like a vapor; she was no longer troubled by dreadful dreams. She was free. She was at last free from heartbreaking disillusionments. She secretly revealed to the middle-age man that her husband left with a much younger woman; a woman she knew and trusted.

Her husband's illness during their marriage and reason for his abandonment were a hidden narrative. Much later however, she discovered that the young woman quickly left her husband when he was sick and incapable of taking care of himself and soon afterwards, he died unaided.

The town's people never knew how and why her husband abruptly left after years of marriage; some thought that her husband died while out of town and others assumed he was placed in a nursing home after a long illness. Back then, though, her husband was a notable town's preacher and highly respected and consequently she refused to inform the town's people about her husband's secret love affair. Years later, however, another secret materialized after the middle-aged women died and left a transcribed and authentic will to her new husband, the middle-aged man who was now an old man. The Black community as well as the White community never knew who owned most of the downtown rental property because they always paid their payments to a distinguished law firm. This information was never disclosed to anyone because of racial prejudice and hatred of Black people and besides so much of the surrounding town's land was given to her by her White great grandfather.

Ironically, it is the same acreage where slaves were beaten, worked, prayed, picked cotton and died. Currently, a local Black college now is located on that land which was donated by the middle-aged man after he died. This narrative became known after the middle-aged man's great grandson became the president of what is now a distinguished Black university.

The Tree of 1944

This is a story about a prominent elderly White woman's paradoxical life-world, social dilemma and racial identity; she was able to navigate between two disconnected worlds that were separated by history, ethnicity and subjugation with absolute self-assurance. While her demeanor persuaded strangers her radiant and youthful eyes and smiles betrayed her aging and frail body. She had no illusions though or infatuations about whom she was. She was passion about her faith and hope of better days, where individuals could live life openly and to the full without pretense. The elderly lady had little choice but to openly perform her role of deception with full coolness, No wonder, she lived all her life in a small town called Hat Creek that strongly adhered to racial taboos and fears

It was a time when a racial caste system was severely enforced and anyone who dared to defy its mores, challenged its institutional structure, or dared to openly flout its laws conclusively and quickly risked his life. To understand these times, Jim Crow was almost a sacred religion and anyone who dared questioned the social order had no choice but to leave town. The population was about 1,200, a place where strange ideas were never appreciated and outsiders were never welcome. For years the elderly lady fought to save an old but dying oak tree against the opinions of most towns' people. Every four or five years someone would raise the issue of cutting down that tree that was in the middle of town and off main street. Older branches from the tree were always falling onto the street and with each passing year a number of leading citizens thought that the old tree was becoming a blot on the landscape and a nuisance to public safety.

Consequently, a number of the town's people began to grumble more overtly and wanted something done about that tree. The only newspaper in town began to print stories about the age and history of that oak tree. In one of the printed articles it was noted that someone had engraved "summer of 1944', but no one really knew the meaning of the etched letters and year. A few of the leading citizens of Hat Creek secretly began to discuss the meaning of the writing on that tree; others however wanted to know why the prominent elderly lady fought for 30 years to save that tree. After all, they reasoned this was 1974 and it was time for a change. By now much younger voices were been heard. Finally the town's people met in one of the local churches to discuss the fate of the old oak tree, a few of the older men however, began to talk about that old oak tree with a sense of nostalgia and noted that the tree symbolized the town's heritage.

But the younger group would not hear of any such talk and sought for a resolution. To everyone surprise, though, the prominent elderly lady stood promptly to her feet and agreed that it was time for that the old dying oak tree to be removed from the town's square, but with one exception though, she exclaimed. The town's people must agree to wait until the end of the summer. At once the town's people all agreed, however a number of them silently wondered as they were leaving the 75 year old church, why the elderly lady lightly and calmly agreed to resign her fight. After more than 30 years the elderly lady had fought with bribes, threats and sometimes, as a few thought, with an authoritarian meanness to save that tree. But now it was all over.

Two months later near the end of the summer a young colored girl about age 12 was walking pass the town's oak tree and saw an elderly Black man sitting on a bench near the tree; she distinctly knew that this was the old man she had secretly heard so much about from the elderly White woman, after all she had been working for the elderly lady for a number of years doing small jobs and doing household tasks. She dropped the packages she was carrying in her arms and excitedly ran to the elderly lady house and abruptly stopped at the front doorway to get her-self under self-control. The old lady came to the front door and asked the girl what was wrong and observed that she looked as if she had seen a ghost.

The girl finally explained that the old man she saw sitting by the oak tree looked just like the man in the photos that was shown to her by the elderly woman. The elderly lady smiled softly and sent the girl home and told her not to mention the man to anyone. The elderly lady leisurely went back into her house knowing now that she would have to leave her town and the few friends she loved. It was now impossible to stay and encounter meanness and hatred from the town's people, if not outright brutality. The elderly lady faced a dilemma that was cautiously protected and precariously safeguarded for years; she was now more acutely aware that the town's people would never accept the reality of her living with a Black man. The thought of staying there in that small town and enjoying a long and healthy life was treacherous at best.

Thus, the elderly White lady got her purse and gradually glanced around the narrow vestibule and unhurriedly closed the front door and stared about her house as if she would never return. Peacefully she closed

the small white fence and walked towards the old oak tree where the old

colored man was sitting. Their life-world personified one soul and yet

distinct persons that embodied a lived experience of caring, but more

appreciably, an unparalleled caring that was beyond time, social status

and political correctness. As their eyes met, there was silence that lasted

for what seemed an hour; but it was a silence that encompassed 30 years

of secret defiance, third party letters, secret messages, name changes and

hidden narratives.

They had known each other since childhood and to say that they

had a once hastily liaison is disingenuous. Over the years however, they

kept their love alive by the promises they had kept to each other since

childhood. Their promises were like secret pledges; they assisted each

for any number of reasons, anytime and anywhere. Their closeness and

faithfulness may seem strange nowadays but it was not as unusual as one

might think and particularly during the time of Jim Crow. The right to live

and love as one chooses was very fundamental for many individuals back

then. People suffered and died for many things, things we take for granted

today and view them as commonplace. Many varieties of relationships and

life-styles were cautiously guarded back then and outsiders were never

allowed to discover a life-world beyond daily life; only a selected and

trusted few was allowed to witness an underground world where freedom

resided alongside repression.

"It has been a long time" the old man said, "no", she said, "it has

been a very long day". Leaving town they drove across several old and

obsolete bridges that connected the interstate to their new residence and

not far from their daughter's house. No one knew who stayed in touch with them for all those years; but I would deduce that it was someone seen and yet invisible, someone who was unseen and yet visible. Much later, at their new residence, they passively reflected upon their life journey as nothing unusual and understood that they rejected all options.

References

Bray, C. (2007). Dream catcher. *New Statesman*, 136, 4848.

Carr, M. J. (2003). Poetic expression of vigilance. *Qualitative Health Research.* 13, 9.

Denzin, K. N.; Lincoln, S. Y. (2003). *The landscape of qualitative research: Theories and issues.* London. Sage.

Foley, J. M. (2005). From oral performance to paper-text to cyber-edition *Oral Tradition*, 20, 2.

Glesne, C. (1997). That rare feeling: Re-presenting research through poetic transcription. *Qualitative Inquiry*, 3, 2.

Larkin, J. (2007). Portraits of a people: Picturing african americans in the nineteenth century. *Journal of the Early Republic,* 27, 2.

Jennings, M,; Lynn, M. (2005). The house that race built: Critical pedagogy, african american education, and the re-conceptualization of critical race pedagogy. *The Journal of the Social Foundations of Education*, 19, 3-4.

Roth, K. (2006). Deliberation in national and post-national education. *Curriculum Studies*, 38.

Scheler,M. (1967). An Intellectual Portrait. New York Free Press. Sweeney, B. D. (2007). Give me liberty. *Arts and Activities*, 141, 5.

Tsur, R. (2000*)*. Picture poetry, mannerism, and sign relationships. *Poetics Today*.

Willits, A. (2007). Are we coming or going? National Catholic Reporter. 43, 29.